Go Karting

Log Book

GW00500072

Karting Addicts

This log book
belongs to

Name
_____

Address
_____

_____

_____

Home No:
_____

Mobile No:
_____

Emergency contact No:
_____

Next of kin
_____

Blood group
_____

Medical conditions
_____

_____

_____

_____

_____

_____

_____

_____

RACE MEETING

_____

Date: _____ Circuit: _____ Class: _____

Organising club: Championship/series:

_____   _____

Qualifying

Conditions: _____ Tyres used: _____

Tyre pressures: Front: _____ Rear: _____

Kart set up notes: _____

_____

_____

Length of qualifying: _____ Laps completed: _____

Fastest time: _____ On lap: _____ Position on grid: _____

Notes on qualifying

Race 1

Conditions: _____   *Tyres used:* _____

Tyre pressure: Front: _____ *Rear:* _____ *Length of race:* _____

Kart set up notes: _____

_____

_____

Overall Position: _____ *Fastest lap:* _____ *On lap:* _____ *Position in class:* _____

Notes:

Race 2

Conditions: _____   *Tyres used:* _____

Tyre pressure: Front: _____ *Rear:* _____ *Length of race:* _____

Kart set up notes: _____

_____

_____

Overall Position: _____ *Fastest lap:* _____ *On lap:* _____ *Position in class:* _____

Notes:

RACE MEETING

_____

Date: _____   Circuit: _____   Class: _____

Organising club: Championship/series:

_____   _____

Qualifying

Conditions: _____   Tyres used: _____

Tyre pressures: Front: _____   Rear: _____

Kart set up notes: _____

_____

_____

Length of qualifying: _____   Laps completed: _____

Fastest time: _____   On lap: _____   Position on grid: _____

Notes on qualifying

Race 1

Conditions: _____ *Tyres used:* _____

Tyre pressure: Front: _____ *Rear:* _____ *Length of race:* _____

Kart set up notes: _____

_____

_____

Overall Position: _____ *Fastest lap:* _____ *On lap:* _____ *Position in class:* _____

Notes:

Race 2

Conditions: _____ *Tyres used:* _____

Tyre pressure: Front: _____ *Rear:* _____ *Length of race:* _____

Kart set up notes: _____

_____

_____

Overall Position: _____ *Fastest lap:* _____ *On lap:* _____ *Position in class:* _____

Notes:

RACE MEETING

_____

Date: _____ Circuit: _____ Class: _____

Organising club: Championship/series:

_____   _____

Qualifying

Conditions: _____   Tyres used: _____

Tyre pressures: Front: _____   Rear: _____

Kart set up notes: _____

_____

_____

Length of qualifying: _____   Laps completed: _____

Fastest time: _____ On lap: _____ Position on grid: _____

Notes on qualifying

Race 1

Conditions: _____ Tyres used: _____

Tyre pressure: Front: _____ Rear: _____ Length of race: _____

Kart set up notes: _____

_____

_____

Overall Position:_____ Fastest lap:_____ On lap: _____ Position in class:_____

Notes:

Race 2

Conditions: _____ Tyres used: _____

Tyre pressure: Front:_____ Rear: _____ Length of race:_____

Kart set up notes: _____

_____

_____

Overall Position:_____ Fastest lap:_____ On lap: _____ Position in class:_____

Notes:

RACE MEETING

_____

Date: _____   Circuit: _____   Class: _____

Organising club: _____   Championship/series: _____

_____   _____

Qualifying

Conditions: _____   Tyres used: _____

Tyre pressures: Front: _____   Rear: _____

Kart set up notes: _____

_____

_____

Length of qualifying: _____   Laps completed: _____

Fastest time: _____   On lap: _____   Position on grid: _____

Notes on qualifying

Race 1

Conditions: _____ *Tyres used:* _____

Tyre pressure: Front: _____ *Rear:* _____ *Length of race:* _____

Kart set up notes: _____

_____

_____

Overall Position: _____ *Fastest lap:* _____ *On lap:* _____ *Position in class:* _____

Notes:

Race 2

Conditions: _____ *Tyres used:* _____

Tyre pressure: Front: _____ *Rear:* _____ *Length of race:* _____

Kart set up notes: _____

_____

_____

Overall Position: _____ *Fastest lap:* _____ *On lap:* _____ *Position in class:* _____

Notes:

RACE MEETING

_____

Date: _____ Circuit: _____ Class: _____

Organising club: Championship/series:

_____   _____

Qualifying

Conditions: _____ Tyres used: _____

Tyre pressures: Front: _____ Rear: _____

Kart set up notes: _____

_____

_____

Length of qualifying: _____ Laps completed: _____

Fastest time: _____ On lap: _____ Position on grid: _____

Notes on qualifying

Race 1

Conditions: _____   Tyres used: _____

Tyre pressure: Front: _____ Rear: _____ Length of race: _____

Kart set up notes:_____

_____

_____

Overall Position:_____ Fastest lap:_____ On lap:_____ Position in class:_____

Notes:

Race 2

Conditions: _____   Tyres used: _____

Tyre pressure: Front:_____ Rear: _____ Length of race:_____

Kart set up notes: _____

_____

_____

Overall Position:_____ Fastest lap:_____ On lap:_____ Position in class:_____

Notes:

RACE MEETING

_____

Date: _____ Circuit: _____ Class: _____

Organising club: Championship/series:

_____   _____

Qualifying

Conditions: _____   Tyres used: _____

Tyre pressures: Front: _____   Rear: _____

Kart set up notes: _____

_____

_____

Length of qualifying: _____   Laps completed: _____

Fastest time: _____ On lap: _____ Position on grid: _____

Notes on qualifying

Race 1

Conditions: _____   Tyres used: _____

Tyre pressure: Front: _____ Rear: _____ Length of race: _____

Kart set up notes: _____

_____

_____

Overall Position: _____ Fastest lap: _____ On lap: _____ Position in class: _____

Notes:

Race 2

Conditions: _____   Tyres used: _____

Tyre pressure: Front: _____ Rear: _____ Length of race: _____

Kart set up notes: _____

_____

_____

Overall Position: _____ Fastest lap: _____ On lap: _____ Position in class: _____

Notes:

RACE MEETING

_____

Date: _____ Circuit: _____ Class: _____

Organising club: Championship/series:

_____   _____

Qualifying

Conditions: _____   Tyres used: _____

Tyre pressures: Front: _____   Rear: _____

Kart set up notes: _____

_____

_____

Length of qualifying: _____   Laps completed: _____

Fastest time: _____ On lap: _____ Position on grid: _____

Notes on qualifying

Race 1

Conditions: _____   Tyres used: _____

Tyre pressure: Front: _____ Rear: _____ Length of race: _____

Kart set up notes:_____

_____

_____

Overall Position:_____ Fastest lap:_____ On lap:_____ Position in class:____

Notes:

Race 2

Conditions: _____   Tyres used: _____

Tyre pressure: Front:_____ Rear: _____ Length of race:_____

Kart set up notes: _____

_____

_____

Overall Position:_____ Fastest lap:_____ On lap:_____ Position in class:____

Notes:

RACE MEETING

_____

Date: _____ Circuit: _____ Class: _____

Organising club: Championship/series:

_____   _____

Qualifying

Conditions: _____   Tyres used: _____

Tyre pressures: Front: _____   Rear: _____

Kart set up notes: _____

_____

_____

Length of qualifying: _____   Laps completed: _____

Fastest time: _____ On lap: _____ Position on grid: _____

Notes on qualifying

Race 1

Conditions: _____   Tyres used: _____

Tyre pressure: Front: _____ Rear: _____ Length of race: _____

Kart set up notes: _____

_____

_____

Overall Position: _____ Fastest lap: _____ On lap: _____ Position in class: _____

Notes:

Race 2

Conditions: _____   Tyres used: _____

Tyre pressure: Front: _____ Rear: _____ Length of race: _____

Kart set up notes: _____

_____

_____

Overall Position: _____ Fastest lap: _____ On lap: _____ Position in class: _____

Notes:

RACE MEETING

_____

Date: _____ Circuit: _____ Class: _____

Organising club: _____ Championship/series: _____

_____ _____

Qualifying

Conditions: _____ Tyres used: _____

Tyre pressures: Front: _____ Rear: _____

Kart set up notes: _____

_____

_____

Length of qualifying: _____ Laps completed: _____

Fastest time: _____ On lap: _____ Position on grid: _____

Notes on qualifying

Race 1

Conditions: _____   Tyres used: _____

Tyre pressure: Front: _____ Rear: _____ Length of race: _____

Kart set up notes: _____

_____

_____

Overall Position:_____ Fastest lap:_____ On lap:_____ Position in class:_____

Notes:

Race 2

Conditions: _____   Tyres used: _____

Tyre pressure: Front:_____ Rear: _____ Length of race:_____

Kart set up notes: _____

_____

_____

Overall Position:_____ Fastest lap:_____ On lap:_____ Position in class:_____

Notes:

RACE MEETING

_____

Date: _____ Circuit: _____ Class: _____

Organising club: Championship/series:

_____   _____

Qualifying

Conditions: _____ Tyres used: _____

Tyre pressures: Front: _____ Rear: _____

Kart set up notes: _____

_____

_____

Length of qualifying: _____ Laps completed: _____

Fastest time: _____ On lap: _____ Position on grid: _____

Notes on qualifying

Race 1

Conditions: _____   Tyres used: _____

Tyre pressure: Front: _____ Rear: _____ Length of race: _____

Kart set up notes:_____

_____

_____

Overall Position:_____ Fastest lap:_____ On lap:_____ Position in class:____

Notes:

Race 2

Conditions: _____   Tyres used: _____

Tyre pressure: Front:_____ Rear: _____ Length of race:_____

Kart set up notes: _____

_____

_____

Overall Position:_____ Fastest lap:_____ On lap:_____ Position in class:____

Notes:

RACE MEETING

_____

Date: _____   Circuit: _____   Class: _____

Organising club: Championship/series:

_____   _____

Qualifying

Conditions: _____   Tyres used: _____

Tyre pressures: Front: _____   Rear: _____

Kart set up notes: _____

_____

_____

Length of qualifying: _____   Laps completed: _____

Fastest time: _____   On lap: _____   Position on grid: _____

Notes on qualifying

Race 1

Conditions: _____ *Tyres used:* _____

Tyre pressure: Front: _____ *Rear:* _____ *Length of race:* _____

Kart set up notes: _____

_____

_____

Overall Position: _____ *Fastest lap:* _____ *On lap:* _____ *Position in class:* _____

Notes:

Race 2

Conditions: _____ *Tyres used:* _____

Tyre pressure: Front: _____ *Rear:* _____ *Length of race:* _____

Kart set up notes: _____

_____

_____

Overall Position: _____ *Fastest lap:* _____ *On lap:* _____ *Position in class:* _____

Notes:

RACE MEETING

_____

Date: _____ Circuit: _____ Class: _____

Organising club: Championship/series:

_____   _____

Qualifying

Conditions: _____   Tyres used: _____

Tyre pressures: Front: _____   Rear: _____

Kart set up notes: _____

_____

_____

Length of qualifying: _____   Laps completed: _____

Fastest time: _____ On lap: _____ Position on grid: _____

Notes on qualifying

Race 1

Conditions: _____   *Tyres used:* _____

Tyre pressure: Front: _____ *Rear:* _____ *Length of race:* _____

Kart set up notes: _____

_____

_____

Overall Position: _____ *Fastest lap:* _____ *On lap:* _____ *Position in class:* _____

Notes:

Race 2

Conditions: _____   *Tyres used:* _____

Tyre pressure: Front: _____ *Rear:* _____ *Length of race:* _____

Kart set up notes: _____

_____

_____

Overall Position: _____ *Fastest lap:* _____ *On lap:* _____ *Position in class:* _____

Notes:

RACE MEETING

_____

Date: _____ *Circuit:* _____ *Class:* _____

Organising club: *Championship/series:*

_____   _____

Qualifying

Conditions: _____   *Tyres used:* _____

Tyre pressures: *Front:* _____   *Rear:* _____

Kart set up notes: _____

_____

_____

Length of qualifying: _____   *Laps completed:* _____

Fastest time: _____ *On lap:* _____ *Position on grid:* _____

Notes on qualifying

Race 1

Conditions: _____ Tyres used: _____

Tyre pressure: Front: _____ Rear: _____ Length of race: _____

Kart set up notes: _____

_____

_____

Overall Position: _____ Fastest lap: _____ On lap: _____ Position in class: _____

Notes:

Race 2

Conditions: _____ Tyres used: _____

Tyre pressure: Front: _____ Rear: _____ Length of race: _____

Kart set up notes: _____

_____

_____

Overall Position: _____ Fastest lap: _____ On lap: _____ Position in class: _____

Notes:

RACE MEETING

_____

Date: _____ *Circuit:* _____ *Class:* _____

Organising club: *Championship/series:*

_____   _____

Qualifying

Conditions: _____   *Tyres used:* _____

Tyre pressures: *Front:* _____   *Rear:* _____

Kart set up notes: _____

_____

_____

Length of qualifying: _____   *Laps completed:* _____

Fastest time: _____ *On lap:* _____ *Position on grid:* _____

Notes on qualifying

Race 1

Conditions: _____   *Tyres used:* _____

Tyre pressure: Front: _____ *Rear:* _____ *Length of race:* _____

Kart set up notes: _____

_____

_____

Overall Position: _____ *Fastest lap:* _____ *On lap:* _____ *Position in class:* _____

Notes:

Race 2

Conditions: _____   *Tyres used:* _____

Tyre pressure: Front: _____ *Rear:* _____ *Length of race:* _____

Kart set up notes: _____

_____

_____

Overall Position: _____ *Fastest lap:* _____ *On lap:* _____ *Position in class:* _____

Notes:

RACE MEETING

_____

Date: _____ Circuit: _____ Class: _____

Organising club: Championship/series:

_____   _____

Qualifying

Conditions: _____   Tyres used: _____

Tyre pressures: Front: _____   Rear: _____

Kart set up notes: _____

_____

_____

Length of qualifying: _____   Laps completed: _____

Fastest time: _____ On lap: _____ Position on grid: _____

Notes on qualifying

Race 1

Conditions: _____   Tyres used: _____

Tyre pressure: Front: _____ Rear: _____ Length of race: _____

Kart set up notes: _____

_____

_____

Overall Position:_____ Fastest lap:_____ On lap:_____ Position in class:_____

Notes:

Race 2

Conditions: _____   Tyres used: _____

Tyre pressure: Front:_____ Rear: _____ Length of race:_____

Kart set up notes: _____

_____

_____

Overall Position:_____ Fastest lap:_____ On lap:_____ Position in class:_____

Notes:

RACE MEETING

_____

Date: _____   Circuit: _____   Class: _____

Organising club: Championship/series:

_____   _____

Qualifying

Conditions: _____   Tyres used: _____

Tyre pressures: Front: _____   Rear: _____

Kart set up notes: _____

_____

_____

Length of qualifying: _____   Laps completed: _____

Fastest time: _____   On lap: _____   Position on grid: _____

Notes on qualifying

Race 1

Conditions: _____   *Tyres used:* _____

Tyre pressure: Front: _____ *Rear:* _____ *Length of race:* _____

Kart set up notes: _____

_____

_____

Overall Position: _____ *Fastest lap:* _____ *On lap:* _____ *Position in class:* _____

Notes:

Race 2

Conditions: _____   *Tyres used:* _____

Tyre pressure: Front: _____ *Rear:* _____ *Length of race:* _____

Kart set up notes: _____

_____

_____

Overall Position: _____ *Fastest lap:* _____ *On lap:* _____ *Position in class:* _____

Notes:

RACE MEETING

_____

Date: _____ Circuit: _____ Class: _____

Organising club: Championship/series:

_____   _____

Qualifying

Conditions: _____   Tyres used: _____

Tyre pressures: Front: _____   Rear: _____

Kart set up notes: _____

_____

_____

Length of qualifying: _____   Laps completed: _____

Fastest time: _____ On lap: _____ Position on grid: _____

Notes on qualifying

Race 1

Conditions: _____   Tyres used: _____

Tyre pressure: Front: _____ Rear: _____ Length of race: _____

Kart set up notes: _____

_____

_____

Overall Position: _____ Fastest lap: _____ On lap: _____ Position in class: _____

Notes:

Race 2

Conditions: _____   Tyres used: _____

Tyre pressure: Front: _____ Rear: _____ Length of race: _____

Kart set up notes: _____

_____

_____

Overall Position: _____ Fastest lap: _____ On lap: _____ Position in class: _____

Notes:

RACE MEETING

_____

Date: _____ Circuit: _____ Class: _____

Organising club: Championship/series:

_____   _____

Qualifying

Conditions: _____   Tyres used: _____

Tyre pressures: Front: _____   Rear: _____

Kart set up notes: _____

_____

_____

Length of qualifying: _____   Laps completed: _____

Fastest time: _____ On lap: _____ Position on grid: _____

Notes on qualifying

Race 1

Conditions: _____   *Tyres used:* _____

Tyre pressure: Front: _____ *Rear:* _____ *Length of race:* _____

Kart set up notes: _____

_____

_____

Overall Position: _____ *Fastest lap:* _____ *On lap:* _____ *Position in class:* _____

Notes:

Race 2

Conditions: _____   *Tyres used:* _____

Tyre pressure: Front: _____ *Rear:* _____ *Length of race:* _____

Kart set up notes: _____

_____

_____

Overall Position: _____ *Fastest lap:* _____ *On lap:* _____ *Position in class:* _____

Notes:

RACE MEETING

_____

Date: _____ Circuit: _____ Class: _____

Organising club: Championship/series:

_____   _____

Qualifying

Conditions: _____   Tyres used: _____

Tyre pressures: Front: _____   Rear: _____

Kart set up notes: _____

_____

_____

Length of qualifying: _____   Laps completed: _____

Fastest time: _____ On lap: _____ Position on grid: _____

Notes on qualifying

Race 1

Conditions: _____   *Tyres used:* _____

Tyre pressure: Front: _____ *Rear:* _____ *Length of race:* _____

Kart set up notes: _____

_____

_____

Overall Position: _____ *Fastest lap:* _____ *On lap:* _____ *Position in class:* _____

Notes:

Race 2

Conditions: _____   *Tyres used:* _____

Tyre pressure: Front: _____ *Rear:* _____ *Length of race:* _____

Kart set up notes: _____

_____

_____

Overall Position: _____ *Fastest lap:* _____ *On lap:* _____ *Position in class:* _____

Notes:

RACE MEETING

_____

Date: _____   Circuit: _____   Class: _____

Organising club: Championship/series:

_____   _____

Qualifying

Conditions: _____   Tyres used: _____

Tyre pressures: Front: _____   Rear: _____

Kart set up notes: _____

_____

_____

Length of qualifying: _____   Laps completed: _____

Fastest time: _____   On lap: _____   Position on grid: _____

Notes on qualifying

Race 1

Conditions: _____ Tyres used: _____

Tyre pressure: Front: _____ Rear: _____ Length of race: _____

Kart set up notes: _____

_____

_____

Overall Position:_____ Fastest lap:_____ On lap:_____ Position in class:_____

Notes:

Race 2

Conditions: _____ Tyres used: _____

Tyre pressure: Front:_____ Rear: _____ Length of race:_____

Kart set up notes: _____

_____

_____

Overall Position:_____ Fastest lap:_____ On lap:_____ Position in class:_____

Notes:

RACE MEETING

_____

Date: _____ Circuit: _____ Class: _____

Organising club: Championship/series:

_____   _____

Qualifying

Conditions: _____   Tyres used: _____

Tyre pressures: Front: _____   Rear: _____

Kart set up notes: _____

_____

_____

Length of qualifying: _____   Laps completed: _____

Fastest time: _____ On lap: _____ Position on grid: _____

Notes on qualifying

Race 1

Conditions: _____   Tyres used: _____

Tyre pressure: Front: _____ Rear: _____ Length of race: _____

Kart set up notes: _____

_____

_____

Overall Position:_____ Fastest lap:_____ On lap:_____ Position in class:_____

Notes:

Race 2

Conditions: _____   Tyres used: _____

Tyre pressure: Front:_____ Rear: _____ Length of race:_____

Kart set up notes: _____

_____

_____

Overall Position:_____ Fastest lap:_____ On lap:_____ Position in class:_____

Notes:

RACE MEETING

_____

Date: _____   Circuit: _____   Class: _____

Organising club: Championship/series:

_____   _____

Qualifying

Conditions: _____   Tyres used: _____

Tyre pressures: Front: _____   Rear: _____

Kart set up notes: _____

_____

_____

Length of qualifying: _____   Laps completed: _____

Fastest time: _____   On lap: _____   Position on grid: _____

Notes on qualifying

Race 1

Conditions: _____   Tyres used: _____

Tyre pressure: Front: _____ Rear: _____ Length of race: _____

Kart set up notes: _____

_____

_____

Overall Position: _____ Fastest lap: _____ On lap: _____ Position in class: _____

Notes:

Race 2

Conditions: _____   Tyres used: _____

Tyre pressure: Front: _____ Rear: _____ Length of race: _____

Kart set up notes: _____

_____

_____

Overall Position: _____ Fastest lap: _____ On lap: _____ Position in class: _____

Notes:

RACE MEETING

_____

Date: _____ Circuit: _____ Class: _____

Organising club: Championship/series:

_____   _____

Qualifying

Conditions: _____   Tyres used: _____

Tyre pressures: Front: _____   Rear: _____

Kart set up notes: _____

_____

_____

Length of qualifying: _____   Laps completed: _____

Fastest time: _____ On lap: _____ Position on grid: _____

Notes on qualifying

Race 1

Conditions: _____   Tyres used: _____

Tyre pressure: Front: _____ Rear: _____ Length of race: _____

Kart set up notes: _____

_____

_____

Overall Position: _____ Fastest lap: _____ On lap: _____ Position in class: _____

Notes:

Race 2

Conditions: _____   Tyres used: _____

Tyre pressure: Front: _____ Rear: _____ Length of race: _____

Kart set up notes: _____

_____

_____

Overall Position: _____ Fastest lap: _____ On lap: _____ Position in class: _____

Notes:

RACE MEETING

_____

Date: _____ Circuit: _____ Class: _____

Organising club: Championship/series:

_____   _____

Qualifying

Conditions: _____   Tyres used: _____

Tyre pressures: Front: _____   Rear: _____

Kart set up notes: _____

_____

_____

Length of qualifying: _____   Laps completed: _____

Fastest time: _____ On lap: _____ Position on grid: _____

Notes on qualifying

Race 1

Conditions: _____   Tyres used: _____

Tyre pressure: Front: _____ Rear: _____ Length of race:_____

Kart set up notes:_____

_____

_____

Overall Position:_____ Fastest lap:_____ On lap:_____ Position in class:_____

Notes:

Race 2

Conditions: _____   Tyres used: _____

Tyre pressure: Front:_____ Rear: _____ Length of race:_____

Kart set up notes: _____

_____

_____

Overall Position:_____ Fastest lap:_____ On lap:_____ Position in class:_____

Notes:

RACE MEETING

_____

Date: _____ Circuit: _____ Class: _____

Organising club: Championship/series:

_____   _____

Qualifying

Conditions: _____ Tyres used: _____

Tyre pressures: Front: _____ Rear: _____

Kart set up notes: _____

_____

_____

Length of qualifying: _____ Laps completed: _____

Fastest time: _____ On lap: _____ Position on grid: _____

Notes on qualifying

Race 1

Conditions: _____ Tyres used: _____

Tyre pressure: Front: _____ Rear: _____ Length of race: _____

Kart set up notes: _____

_____

_____

Overall Position: _____ Fastest lap: _____ On lap: _____ Position in class: _____

Notes:

Race 2

Conditions: _____ Tyres used: _____

Tyre pressure: Front: _____ Rear: _____ Length of race: _____

Kart set up notes: _____

_____

_____

Overall Position: _____ Fastest lap: _____ On lap: _____ Position in class: _____

Notes:

RACE MEETING

_____

Date: _____ _Circuit:_ _____ _Class:_ _____

Organising club: _Championship/series:_

_____   _____

Qualifying

Conditions: _____   _Tyres used:_ _____

Tyre pressures: _Front:_ _____   _Rear:_ _____

Kart set up notes: _____

_____

_____

Length of qualifying: _____   _Laps completed:_ _____

Fastest time: _____ _On lap:_ _____ _Position on grid:_ _____

Notes on qualifying

Race 1

Conditions: _____   Tyres used: _____

Tyre pressure: Front: _____   Rear: _____   Length of race: _____

Kart set up notes: _____

_____

_____

Overall Position: _____ Fastest lap: _____ On lap: _____ Position in class: _____

Notes:

Race 2

Conditions: _____   Tyres used: _____

Tyre pressure: Front: _____   Rear: _____   Length of race: _____

Kart set up notes: _____

_____

_____

Overall Position: _____ Fastest lap: _____ On lap: _____ Position in class: _____

Notes:

RACE MEETING

_____

Date: _____ Circuit: _____ Class: _____

Organising club: Championship/series:

_____   _____

Qualifying

Conditions: _____   Tyres used: _____

Tyre pressures: Front: _____   Rear: _____

Kart set up notes: _____

_____

_____

Length of qualifying: _____   Laps completed: _____

Fastest time: _____ On lap: _____ Position on grid: _____

Notes on qualifying

Race 1

Conditions: _____   Tyres used: _____

Tyre pressure: Front: _____ Rear: _____ Length of race:_____

Kart set up notes:_____

_____

_____

Overall Position:_____ Fastest lap:_____ On lap:_____Position in class:_____

Notes:

Race 2

Conditions: _____   Tyres used: _____

Tyre pressure: Front:_____ Rear: _____ Length of race:_____

Kart set up notes: _____

_____

_____

Overall Position:_____ Fastest lap:_____ On lap:_____Position in class:_____

Notes:

RACE MEETING

_____

Date: _____ Circuit: _____ Class: _____

Organising club: Championship/series:

_____   _____

Qualifying

Conditions: _____   Tyres used: _____

Tyre pressures: Front: _____   Rear: _____

Kart set up notes: _____

_____

_____

Length of qualifying: _____   Laps completed: _____

Fastest time: _____ On lap: _____ Position on grid: _____

Notes on qualifying

Race 1

Conditions: _____ Tyres used: _____

Tyre pressure: Front: _____ Rear: _____ Length of race: _____

Kart set up notes: _____

_____

_____

Overall Position: _____ Fastest lap: _____ On lap: _____ Position in class: _____

Notes:

Race 2

Conditions: _____ Tyres used: _____

Tyre pressure: Front: _____ Rear: _____ Length of race: _____

Kart set up notes: _____

_____

_____

Overall Position: _____ Fastest lap: _____ On lap: _____ Position in class: _____

Notes:

RACE MEETING

_____

Date: _____   Circuit: _____   Class: _____

Organising club: Championship/series:

_____   _____

Qualifying

Conditions: _____   Tyres used: _____

Tyre pressures: Front: _____   Rear: _____

Kart set up notes: _____

_____

_____

Length of qualifying: _____   Laps completed: _____

Fastest time: _____ On lap: _____ Position on grid: _____

Notes on qualifying

Race 1

Conditions: _____ Tyres used: _____

Tyre pressure: Front: _____ Rear: _____ Length of race:_____

Kart set up notes:_____

_____

_____

Overall Position:_____ Fastest lap:_____ On lap:_____ Position in class:_____

Notes:

Race 2

Conditions: _____ Tyres used: _____

Tyre pressure: Front:_____ Rear: _____ Length of race:_____

Kart set up notes: _____

_____

_____

Overall Position:_____ Fastest lap:_____ On lap: _____ Position in class:_____

Notes:

RACE MEETING

_____

Date: _____ Circuit: _____ Class: _____

Organising club: Championship/series:

_____   _____

Qualifying

Conditions: _____   Tyres used: _____

Tyre pressures: Front: _____   Rear: _____

Kart set up notes: _____

_____

_____

Length of qualifying: _____   Laps completed: _____

Fastest time: _____ On lap: _____ Position on grid: _____

Notes on qualifying

Race 1

Conditions: _____   *Tyres used:* _____

Tyre pressure: Front: _____ *Rear:* _____ *Length of race:* _____

Kart set up notes: _____

_____

_____

Overall Position: _____ *Fastest lap:* _____ *On lap:* _____ *Position in class:* _____

Notes:

Race 2

Conditions: _____   *Tyres used:* _____

Tyre pressure: Front: _____ *Rear:* _____ *Length of race:* _____

Kart set up notes: _____

_____

_____

Overall Position: _____ *Fastest lap:* _____ *On lap:* _____ *Position in class:* _____

Notes:

RACE MEETING

_____

Date: _____ Circuit: _____ Class: _____

Organising club: Championship/series:

_____   _____

Qualifying

Conditions: _____ Tyres used: _____

Tyre pressures: Front: _____ Rear: _____

Kart set up notes: _____

_____

_____

Length of qualifying: _____ Laps completed: _____

Fastest time: _____ On lap: _____ Position on grid: _____

Notes on qualifying

Race 1

Conditions: _____   Tyres used: _____

Tyre pressure: Front: _____ Rear: _____ Length of race: _____

Kart set up notes: _____

_____

_____

Overall Position: _____ Fastest lap: _____ On lap: _____ Position in class: _____

Notes:

Race 2

Conditions: _____   Tyres used: _____

Tyre pressure: Front: _____ Rear: _____ Length of race: _____

Kart set up notes: _____

_____

_____

Overall Position: _____ Fastest lap: _____ On lap: _____ Position in class: _____

Notes:

RACE MEETING

_____

Date: _____ Circuit: _____ Class: _____

Organising club: Championship/series:

_____   _____

Qualifying

Conditions: _____   Tyres used: _____

Tyre pressures: Front: _____   Rear: _____

Kart set up notes: _____

_____

_____

Length of qualifying: _____   Laps completed: _____

Fastest time: _____ On lap: _____ Position on grid: _____

Notes on qualifying

Race 1

Conditions: _____   Tyres used: _____

Tyre pressure: Front: _____ Rear: _____ Length of race: _____

Kart set up notes: _____

_____

_____

Overall Position:_____ Fastest lap:_____ On lap:_____ Position in class:____

Notes:

Race 2

Conditions: _____   Tyres used: _____

Tyre pressure: Front:_____ Rear: _____ Length of race:_____

Kart set up notes: _____

_____

_____

Overall Position:_____ Fastest lap:_____ On lap:_____ Position in class:____

Notes:

RACE MEETING

_____

Date: _____ Circuit: _____ Class: _____

Organising club: _____ Championship/series: _____

_____

Qualifying

Conditions: _____ Tyres used: _____

Tyre pressures: Front: _____ Rear: _____

Kart set up notes: _____

_____

_____

Length of qualifying: _____ Laps completed: _____

Fastest time: _____ On lap: _____ Position on grid: _____

Notes on qualifying

Race 1

Conditions: _____   Tyres used: _____

Tyre pressure: Front: _____ Rear: _____ Length of race: _____

Kart set up notes: _____

_____

_____

Overall Position: _____ Fastest lap: _____ On lap: _____ Position in class: _____

Notes:

Race 2

Conditions: _____   Tyres used: _____

Tyre pressure: Front: _____ Rear: _____ Length of race: _____

Kart set up notes: _____

_____

_____

Overall Position: _____ Fastest lap: _____ On lap: _____ Position in class: _____

Notes:

RACE MEETING

_____

Date: _____ _Circuit:_ _____ _Class:_ _____

Organising club: _Championship/series:_

_____   _____

Qualifying

Conditions: _____   _Tyres used:_ _____

Tyre pressures: _Front:_ _____   _Rear:_ _____

Kart set up notes: _____

_____

_____

Length of qualifying: _____   _Laps completed:_ _____

Fastest time: _____ _On lap:_ _____ _Position on grid:_ _____

Notes on qualifying

Race 1

Conditions: _____   Tyres used: _____

Tyre pressure: Front: _____ Rear: _____ Length of race: _____

Kart set up notes: _____

_____

_____

Overall Position:_____ Fastest lap:_____ On lap: _____ Position in class:_____

Notes:

Race 2

Conditions: _____   Tyres used: _____

Tyre pressure: Front: _____ Rear: _____ Length of race: _____

Kart set up notes: _____

_____

_____

Overall Position:_____ Fastest lap:_____ On lap: _____ Position in class:_____

Notes:

RACE MEETING

_____

Date: _____   Circuit: _____   Class: _____

Organising club: Championship/series:

_____   _____

Qualifying

Conditions: _____   Tyres used: _____

Tyre pressures: Front: _____   Rear: _____

Kart set up notes: _____

_____

_____

Length of qualifying: _____   Laps completed: _____

Fastest time: _____   On lap: _____   Position on grid: _____

Notes on qualifying

Race 1

Conditions: _____ Tyres used: _____

Tyre pressure: Front: _____ Rear: _____ Length of race: _____

Kart set up notes: _____

_____

_____

Overall Position: _____ Fastest lap: _____ On lap: _____ Position in class: _____

Notes:

Race 2

Conditions: _____ Tyres used: _____

Tyre pressure: Front: _____ Rear: _____ Length of race: _____

Kart set up notes: _____

_____

_____

Overall Position: _____ Fastest lap: _____ On lap: _____ Position in class: _____

Notes:

RACE MEETING

_____

Date: _____   Circuit: _____   Class: _____

Organising club: Championship/series:

_____   _____

Qualifying

Conditions: _____   Tyres used: _____

Tyre pressures: Front: _____   Rear: _____

Kart set up notes: _____

_____

_____

Length of qualifying: _____   Laps completed: _____

Fastest time: _____   On lap: _____   Position on grid: _____

Notes on qualifying

Race 1

Conditions: _____   Tyres used: _____

Tyre pressure: Front: _____ Rear: _____ Length of race: _____

Kart set up notes: _____

_____

_____

Overall Position:_____ Fastest lap:_____ On lap:_____ Position in class:_____

Notes:

Race 2

Conditions: _____   Tyres used: _____

Tyre pressure: Front:_____ Rear: _____ Length of race: _____

Kart set up notes: _____

_____

_____

Overall Position:_____ Fastest lap:_____ On lap: _____ Position in class:_____

Notes:

RACE MEETING

_____

Date: _____ *Circuit:* _____ *Class:* _____

Organising club: *Championship/series:*

_____   _____

Qualifying

Conditions: _____   *Tyres used:* _____

Tyre pressures: *Front:* _____   *Rear:* _____

Kart set up notes: _____

_____

_____

Length of qualifying: _____   *Laps completed:* _____

Fastest time: _____ *On lap:* _____ *Position on grid:* _____

Notes on qualifying

Race 1

Conditions: _____   Tyres used: _____

Tyre pressure: Front: _____ Rear: _____ Length of race: _____

Kart set up notes: _____

_____

_____

Overall Position: _____ Fastest lap: _____ On lap: _____ Position in class: _____

Notes:

Race 2

Conditions: _____   Tyres used: _____

Tyre pressure: Front: _____ Rear: _____ Length of race: _____

Kart set up notes: _____

_____

_____

Overall Position: _____ Fastest lap: _____ On lap: _____ Position in class: _____

Notes:

RACE MEETING

_____

Date: _____ Circuit: _____ Class: _____

Organising club: Championship/series:

_____   _____

Qualifying

Conditions: _____   Tyres used: _____

Tyre pressures: Front: _____   Rear: _____

Kart set up notes: _____

_____

_____

Length of qualifying: _____   Laps completed: _____

Fastest time: _____ On lap: _____ Position on grid: _____

Notes on qualifying

Race 1

Conditions: _____   Tyres used: _____

Tyre pressure: Front: _____ Rear: _____ Length of race: _____

Kart set up notes: _____

_____

_____

Overall Position: _____ Fastest lap: _____ On lap: _____ Position in class: _____

Notes:

Race 2

Conditions: _____   Tyres used: _____

Tyre pressure: Front: _____ Rear: _____ Length of race: _____

Kart set up notes: _____

_____

_____

Overall Position: _____ Fastest lap: _____ On lap: _____ Position in class: _____

Notes:

RACE MEETING

_____

Date: _____   Circuit: _____   Class: _____

Organising club: _____   Championship/series: _____

_____   _____

Qualifying

Conditions: _____   Tyres used: _____

Tyre pressures: Front: _____   Rear: _____

Kart set up notes: _____

_____

_____

Length of qualifying: _____   Laps completed: _____

Fastest time: _____   On lap: _____   Position on grid: _____

Notes on qualifying

Race 1

Conditions: _____ Tyres used: _____

Tyre pressure: Front: _____ Rear: _____ Length of race: _____

Kart set up notes: _____

_____

_____

Overall Position: _____ Fastest lap: _____ On lap: _____ Position in class: _____

Notes:

Race 2

Conditions: _____ Tyres used: _____

Tyre pressure: Front: _____ Rear: _____ Length of race: _____

Kart set up notes: _____

_____

_____

Overall Position: _____ Fastest lap: _____ On lap: _____ Position in class: _____

Notes:

RACE MEETING

_____

Date: _____   Circuit: _____   Class: _____

Organising club: Championship/series:

_____   _____

Qualifying

Conditions: _____   Tyres used: _____

Tyre pressures: Front: _____   Rear: _____

Kart set up notes: _____

_____

_____

Length of qualifying: _____   Laps completed: _____

Fastest time: _____   On lap: _____   Position on grid: _____

Notes on qualifying

Race 1

Conditions: _____   Tyres used: _____

Tyre pressure: Front: _____ Rear: _____ Length of race: _____

Kart set up notes: _____

_____

_____

Overall Position: _____ Fastest lap: _____ On lap: _____ Position in class: _____

Notes:

Race 2

Conditions: _____   Tyres used: _____

Tyre pressure: Front: _____ Rear: _____ Length of race: _____

Kart set up notes: _____

_____

_____

Overall Position: _____ Fastest lap: _____ On lap: _____ Position in class: _____

Notes:

RACE MEETING

_____

Date: _____ Circuit: _____ Class: _____

Organising club: _____ Championship/series: _____

Qualifying

Conditions: _____ Tyres used: _____

Tyre pressures: Front: _____ Rear: _____

Kart set up notes: _____

_____

_____

Length of qualifying: _____ Laps completed: _____

Fastest time: _____ On lap: _____ Position on grid: _____

Notes on qualifying

Race 1

Conditions: _____ Tyres used: _____

Tyre pressure: Front: _____ Rear: _____ Length of race: _____

Kart set up notes: _____

_____

_____

Overall Position: _____ Fastest lap: _____ On lap: _____ Position in class: _____

Notes:

Race 2

Conditions: _____ Tyres used: _____

Tyre pressure: Front: _____ Rear: _____ Length of race: _____

Kart set up notes: _____

_____

_____

Overall Position: _____ Fastest lap: _____ On lap: _____ Position in class: _____

Notes:

RACE MEETING

_____

Date: _____ Circuit: _____ Class: _____

Organising club: Championship/series:

_____   _____

Qualifying

Conditions: _____   Tyres used: _____

Tyre pressures: Front: _____   Rear: _____

Kart set up notes: _____

_____

_____

Length of qualifying: _____   Laps completed: _____

Fastest time: _____ On lap: _____ Position on grid: _____

Notes on qualifying

Race 1

Conditions: _____ Tyres used: _____

Tyre pressure: Front: _____ Rear: _____ Length of race: _____

Kart set up notes: _____

_____

_____

Overall Position: _____ Fastest lap: _____ On lap: _____ Position in class: _____

Notes:

Race 2

Conditions: _____ Tyres used: _____

Tyre pressure: Front: _____ Rear: _____ Length of race: _____

Kart set up notes: _____

_____

_____

Overall Position: _____ Fastest lap: _____ On lap: _____ Position in class: _____

Notes:

RACE MEETING

_____

Date: _____ Circuit: _____ Class: _____

Organising club: Championship/series:

_____ _____

Qualifying

Conditions: _____ Tyres used: _____

Tyre pressures: Front: _____ Rear: _____

Kart set up notes: _____

_____

_____

Length of qualifying: _____ Laps completed: _____

Fastest time: _____ On lap: _____ Position on grid: _____

Notes on qualifying

Race 1

Conditions: _____   Tyres used: _____

Tyre pressure: Front: _____ Rear: _____ Length of race: _____

Kart set up notes: _____

_____

_____

Overall Position: _____ Fastest lap: _____ On lap: _____ Position in class: _____

Notes:

Race 2

Conditions: _____   Tyres used: _____

Tyre pressure: Front: _____ Rear: _____ Length of race: _____

Kart set up notes: _____

_____

_____

Overall Position: _____ Fastest lap: _____ On lap: _____ Position in class: _____

Notes:

RACE MEETING

_____

Date: _____ Circuit: _____ Class: _____

Organising club: Championship/series:

_____   _____

Qualifying

Conditions: _____   Tyres used: _____

Tyre pressures: Front: _____   Rear: _____

Kart set up notes: _____

_____

_____

Length of qualifying: _____   Laps completed: _____

Fastest time: _____ On lap: _____ Position on grid: _____

Notes on qualifying

Race 1

Conditions: _____   *Tyres used:* _____

Tyre pressure: Front: _____ *Rear:* _____ *Length of race:* _____

Kart set up notes: _____

_____

_____

Overall Position: _____ *Fastest lap:* _____ *On lap:* _____ *Position in class:* _____

Notes:

Race 2

Conditions: _____   *Tyres used:* _____

Tyre pressure: Front: _____ *Rear:* _____ *Length of race:* _____

Kart set up notes: _____

_____

_____

Overall Position: _____ *Fastest lap:* _____ *On lap:* _____ *Position in class:* _____

Notes:

RACE MEETING

_____

Date: _____ Circuit: _____ Class: _____

Organising club: Championship/series:

_____   _____

Qualifying

Conditions: _____   Tyres used: _____

Tyre pressures: Front: _____   Rear: _____

Kart set up notes: _____

_____

_____

Length of qualifying: _____   Laps completed: _____

Fastest time: _____ On lap: _____ Position on grid: _____

Notes on qualifying

Race 1

Conditions: _____   Tyres used: _____

Tyre pressure: Front: _____ Rear: _____ Length of race: _____

Kart set up notes: _____

_____

_____

Overall Position:_____ Fastest lap:_____ On lap:_____ Position in class:_____

Notes:

Race 2

Conditions: _____   Tyres used: _____

Tyre pressure: Front:_____ Rear: _____ Length of race:_____

Kart set up notes: _____

_____

_____

Overall Position:_____ Fastest lap:_____ On lap:_____ Position in class:_____

Notes:

RACE MEETING

_____

Date: _____ Circuit: _____ Class: _____

Organising club: Championship/series:

_____   _____

Qualifying

Conditions: _____   Tyres used: _____

Tyre pressures: Front: _____   Rear: _____

Kart set up notes: _____

_____

_____

Length of qualifying: _____   Laps completed: _____

Fastest time: _____ On lap: _____ Position on grid: _____

Notes on qualifying

Race 1

Conditions: _____   *Tyres used:* _____

Tyre pressure: Front: _____ *Rear:* _____ *Length of race:* _____

Kart set up notes: _____

_____

_____

Overall Position: _____ *Fastest lap:* _____ *On lap:* _____ *Position in class:* _____

Notes:

Race 2

Conditions: _____   *Tyres used:* _____

Tyre pressure: Front: _____ *Rear:* _____ *Length of race:* _____

Kart set up notes: _____

_____

_____

Overall Position: _____ *Fastest lap:* _____ *On lap:* _____ *Position in class:* _____

Notes:

RACE MEETING

_____

Date: _____ Circuit: _____ Class: _____

Organising club: Championship/series:

_____   _____

Qualifying

Conditions: _____ Tyres used: _____

Tyre pressures: Front: _____ Rear: _____

Kart set up notes: _____

_____

_____

Length of qualifying: _____ Laps completed: _____

Fastest time: _____ On lap: _____ Position on grid: _____

Notes on qualifying

Race 1

Conditions: _____ *Tyres used:* _____

Tyre pressure: Front: _____ *Rear:* _____ *Length of race:* _____

Kart set up notes: _____

_____

_____

Overall Position: _____ *Fastest lap:* _____ *On lap:* _____ *Position in class:* _____

Notes:

Race 2

Conditions: _____ *Tyres used:* _____

Tyre pressure: Front: _____ *Rear:* _____ *Length of race:* _____

Kart set up notes: _____

_____

_____

Overall Position: _____ *Fastest lap:* _____ *On lap:* _____ *Position in class:* _____

Notes:

RACE MEETING

_____

Date: _____   Circuit: _____   Class: _____

Organising club: Championship/series:

_____   _____

Qualifying

Conditions: _____   Tyres used: _____

Tyre pressures: Front: _____   Rear: _____

Kart set up notes: _____

_____

_____

Length of qualifying: _____   Laps completed: _____

Fastest time: _____ On lap: _____ Position on grid: _____

Notes on qualifying

Race 1

Conditions: _____   Tyres used: _____

Tyre pressure: Front: _____ Rear: _____ Length of race: _____

Kart set up notes: _____

_____

_____

Overall Position: _____ Fastest lap: _____ On lap: _____ Position in class: _____

Notes:

Race 2

Conditions: _____   Tyres used: _____

Tyre pressure: Front: _____ Rear: _____ Length of race: _____

Kart set up notes: _____

_____

_____

Overall Position: _____ Fastest lap: _____ On lap: _____ Position in class: _____

Notes:

Printed in Great Britain
by Amazon